# Folksongs from Eastern Euro[pe]

## selected and arranged for voices and keyboard by

## KEN AND JEAN BOLAM

©1992 by Faber Music Ltd
First published in 1992 by Faber Music Ltd
3 Queen Square London WC1N 3AU
Illustrations by John Levers
Cover illustration by Angela Dundee
©1992 by Faber Music Ltd
Music processed by Silverfen
Printed in England by Reflex Litho Ltd

ISBN 0 571 51308 5

FABER *ff* MUSIC

# Preface

**Folksongs from Eastern Europe** brings together a wide collection of songs from seven of the countries formerly behind the 'iron curtain' in Europe, including East Germany (designated 'German' here).

Folksongs are a poetic and musical mirror of the life and character of the people from whom they evolve, and we have attempted to choose music typical of the various nationalities as well as from different eras. As in all folksong, variations in melody, lyrics and tempo were encountered, and we have attempted wherever possible to select the 'most popular' version of each.

Many of the songs fall into a verse and chorus pattern (choruses are printed in italic type): it can be effective for a soloist or solo group to sing the verse, and everyone the chorus. The keyboard accompaniments have been kept deliberately simple and chord symbols are provided throughout. Percussion instruments should be used at will, and the melody and chord symbols can be used as a guide for tuned percussion.

Each one of the nationalities represented here is, of course, worthy of its own volume; we hope, however, that this selection will offer an enjoyable taste of the wealth and variety of folk material from the rich heritage of these countries – and that you find as much enjoyment performing the songs as we have had collecting them.

Ken and Jean Bolam

# Contents

# Fairest Katy

Slovak

**Gaily**

1. Fair - est Ka - ty walked out at dawn - ing, She

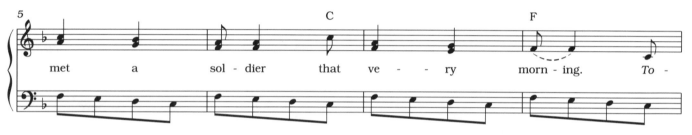

met a sol - dier that ve - - ry morn - ing. To -

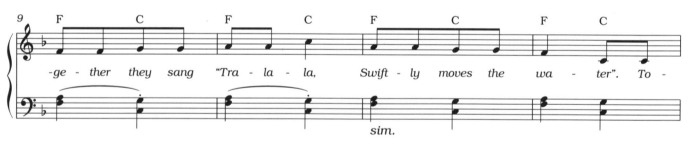

-ge - ther they sang "Tra - la - la, Swift - ly moves the wa - ter". To -

-ge - ther they sang "Tra - la - la, Swift - ly moves the stream".

2. "Let me help you, O pretty maiden,
   Your bag looks heavy, you seem so laden."
   *Together they sang (etc.)*

3. "Thank you, kind sir, but no," said she,
   "It's only goose-down, and light for me."
   *Together they sang (etc.)*

# At the fair

**Cheerfully**

Slovak

1. There is a fair in the field to - night,

Lights are a - shin - ing so clear and bright.

Mu - sic is play - ing, swing - boats are sway - ing,

Peo - ple are smil - ing with pure de - light.

2. "Roll up," the man at the side-show cries,
   "You may be lucky and win a prize."
   Sweet foods invite us, stalls will excite us,
   Round ev'ry corner a new surprise.

3. "Beautiful maiden, fine as can be,
   My dearest love, will you marry me?"
   "O yes, my Johnny, so fair and bonny,
   We shall be wed soon, ah, you shall see."

# The echo of our youth

Bulgarian

**March time**

1. The corn is glis-ten-ing a - round—— us, All shin-ing in the gen-tle sum-mer rains;—— And we go for-ward, we go e-ver, e-ver for - ward,_ In-to the ne-ver-end-ing vis-ta of the plains, And we go for-ward, we go e-ver, e-ver for - ward,_ In-to the ne-ver-end-ing vis-ta of the plains. *Then e - cho,—— then e - cho,—— All bound-less lies the world; Then e - cho,—— then e - cho,—— All bound-less lies the world.*

2. We children of a joyful motherland,
   Come marching from the
        distant field and town;
   ‖: With happy footsteps that are
        ringing through the valleys,
   We'll bear our youthful,
        newborn freedom bravely on. :‖
        ‖: *Then echo, then echo,
        we'll bear our freedom on.* :‖

3. This life of ours can have no limit:
   No limit to our striving and our love.
   ‖: There is no ending to the
        struggle and the progress,
   And to the power
        of our own heroic youth. :‖
        ‖: *Then ring out, then ring out,
        the echo of our youth!* :‖

—4—

# The wedding

2. To the altar now they lead my dear one,
   Now at last, O maiden dearest,
      this time you are mine.
         "No, not quite yet *(etc.)*"

3. From the altar now I lead my dear one,
   Now at last, O maiden dearest,
      this time you are mine.
         "Now I'm thine, O my most belovèd;
         Not my mother's now, but thine!"

# Hurry, the food is ready

Czech

2. Hurry, the food is ready,
   Hurry, and let's begin.
   Cakes are baking in the oven,
   I've put lots of sugar in.

3. Hurry, the food is ready,
   Hurry, and let's begin.
   Chicken's roasting, in the oven,
   I've put herbs and garlic in.

4. Hurry, the food is ready,
   Hurry, and let's begin.
   Bread is baking in the oven,
   I've put lots of currants in.

1. Hur – ry, the food is rea – dy, Hur – ry, and let's be – gin.

Soup is boil – ing in the sauce – pan, I've put lots of car – rots in.

# Single life is over

**Brightly**

Hungarian

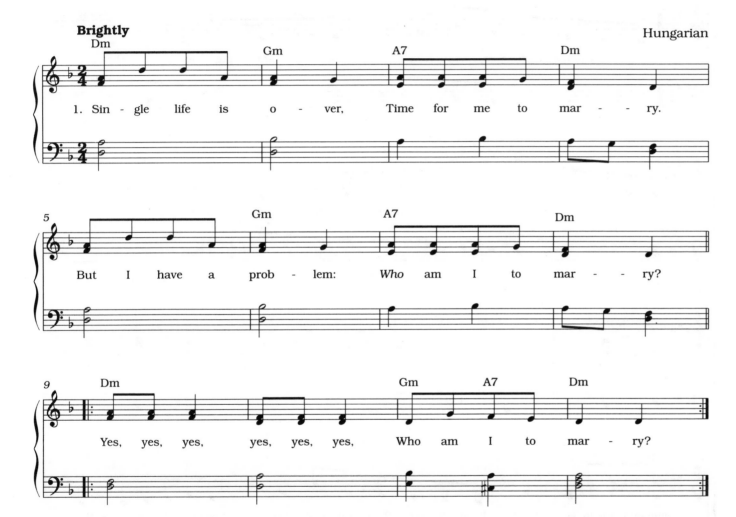

1. Sin - gle life is o - ver, Time for me to mar - ry.

But I have a prob - lem: *Who am I to mar - ry?*

Yes, yes, yes, yes, yes, yes, Who am I to mar - ry?

2. She has to be wealthy,
Has to have some money;
If she has no money
I still have my problem:
Yes, yes, yes, yes, yes, yes,
Who am I to marry?
Yes, yes, yes, yes, yes, yes,
Who am I to marry?

3. If I do not marry,
Will I still be happy?
If I do not marry,
I won't have a problem:
No, no, no, no, no, no,
I won't have a problem.
No, no, no, no, no, no,
I won't have a problem.

# Shoes of shining leather

Hungarian

**Gaily**

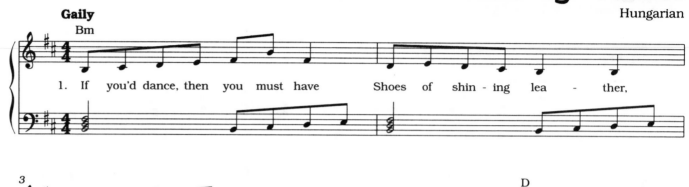

1. If you'd dance, then you must have Shoes of shin-ing lea - ther,

Mo-ney in your pock-et book, In your cap a fea - ther. But if you would

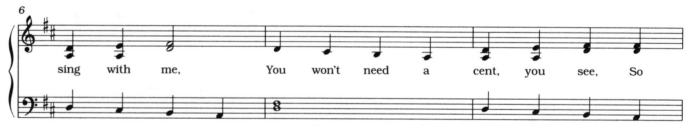

sing with me, You won't need a cent, you see, So

2. If you wed a pretty girl,
   That will cost you money:
   She will want a hundred things,
   Rainy days or sunny.
   But if you would sing with me,
   You won't need a cent, you see.
   So come and sing beside me!
   If you'd wed that pretty girl,
   That will cost you money.

come and sing to-ge - ther! If you'd dance, then you must have shoes of shi-ning lea - ther.

# Take your swords

**Fast and fiery**

Polish

1. Take your swords, O — bro - thers, dar - ing, Let there be re - joic - ing, Po - land's glo - ry — we'll be — shar - ing, Tri - umph we'll be voic - ing. Here's to Po - land's glo - ry, And her ma - jes - tic sto - ry! Here's to Po - land's glo - ry, And her ma - jes - tic sto - ry! sto - ry!

2. Are we not from Cracow County,
Braver than all others?
Polish spirit full of bounty,
Cracow lads are brothers.
*Here's to Poland's glory (etc.)*

3. In the midst of fearsome fighting,
We will stand undaunted;
Though the battle be exciting,
Our deeds won't be flaunted.
*Here's to Poland's glory (etc.)*

# I don't want you near me

Polish

**Moderate**

1. I don't want you near me, Ka-ty—— dear, Peo-ple say bad things a-bout you here:

You rise late, and prat-tle, You don't feed the cat-tle, You don't wake the board-er,

Things are in dis-or-der; No, no, no, no, no!

2. That's not true, dear Johnny,
   that's not true!
   Oh, these folks are cruel
   through and through:
      I don't ever prattle,
      And I feed the cattle,
      And I keep the boarder,
      And keep things in order,
   Yes, yes, yes, yes, yes!

3. If you don't believe me, my own sweet,
   Tie two little bells to both my feet.
      Then when I awaken,
      Both bells will be shaken;
      While I work a-singing
      Both bells will be ringing:
   Ding, ding, ding, ding, ding!

—10—

# The bugle call

**March time**

Westphalian

1. Our hearts are warm as sun-light For the fa-ther-land we love; The clash of swords is mu-sic That has power our souls to move. Our — fa-thers' spi-rit leads us To fight when our coun-try needs us. *But the voice that we love, Ev-'ry voice a-bove, Is the strain that we greet When the foe is there to beat; The mu-sic of the bu-gle, The call that ne-ver sounds re-treat!*

2. The pipe of peace may cheer us,
   To the joys of home we yield,
   But when there's danger near us
   Then our place is on the field.
   Our country's flag waves o'er us,
   And victory lies before us,
       *But the voice that we love, (etc.)*

3. With gun to fit our shoulder,
   And a sword our wrist can ply,
   The foe had need be bolder
   If he thinks to make us fly.
   Tho' shells around us scatter,
   Tho' long the odds, what matters?
       *But the voice that we love, (etc.)*

# Golden fish swimming in the lake

Polish

**Fast (mazurka)**

1. Gol - den fish swim-ming in the lake, So ma - ny fish that we can take,
2. In the clear wa - ter see them dart, Catch - ing them will take all our art,

Let's cross the pur - ple hea - ther, — let's cross the pur - ple hea - ther, —
Come on, lets get our feet wet, — come on, let's get our feet wet; —

Let us go and catch all the fish we can, What - e - ver be the wea - ther;
Ev - en if it rains, John - ny will come out, How ma - ny fish can he get?

Let us go and catch all the fish we can, What - e - ver be the wea - ther.
Ev - en if it rains, John - ny will come out, How ma - ny fish can he get?

# The maid of Leko

German

Slow

1. There lived a mai - den long a - go, Blue - eyed, fair as ⎯ day: Up - on the isle of Hest - man - do Lived this fair maid, And it is said All hearts owed her ⎯ sway.

2. There came a rider, proud and bold;
   To the maid did he plead,
   Yet to his wooing she was cold.
   Coarsely he played
   To the fair maid,
   Riding on his steed.

3. The maiden knew how sad her plight,
   Helpless and alone;
   She prayed to heav'n to aid her flight,
   And in their course
   Rider and horse
   Turned to solid stone.

4. And still the mounted horseman stands
   Upon Leko Hill,
   And people from Norwegian lands
   Bow as they pass,
   Seeing – alas! –
   How rash love works ill.

—13—

# In the hedge there is a little hare

Polish

**Lively**

1. In the hedge there is a lit-tle hare, lit-tle hare, But the hun-ters don't know that he's there, that he's there; They re-lease the dogs and scat-ter, Soon they hear a noi-sy clat-ter: There goes hare! There goes hare!

2. All the hun-ters try to make the catch, make the catch; But the hare is not an ea-sy match, ea-sy match; See him where he hops so light-ly, Dash-ing through the woods, so spright-ly, where he's king, where he's king!

—14—

# Where are the happy dreams of childhood?

**Moderate**

German

1. Where are the hap-py dreams of child-hood, With their love and their truth, Those vi - sions of __ beau-ty That __ daz - zled our __ youth? They passed like the clouds by the morn - ing un - rolled, Be-decked with the glo - ry be - decked with the glo - ry, be-decked with the glo - ry Of crim - son and gold, Be - decked with the glo - ry Of crim - son and gold.

2. Where are the happy dreams of manhood,
   That seemed true and secure?
   So strong and so certain,
   Of success ever sure;
   As we near the mirage
   It sinks in the sand;
   We grasp at the bubble, *(3 times)*
   It bursts in our hand.

3. Let us live in the present,
   There's no truth in our dreams:
   They melt like the rainbow's
   Enchanting beams.
   In youth's morning beauty,
   In manhood, old age,
   The true and the lasting *(3 times)*
   Our thoughts should engage.

—15—

# Goodnight

Czech

*Good-night be-lo-ved, good-night, good-night,*

*God keep you safe in his watch-ful sight.* 1. Good-night, dear, soft-ly sleep:

Sweet be the dreams of your slum-ber deep. Good-night, dear, soft-ly sleep:

Sweet be the dreams of your slum-ber deep.

2. Goodnight, dear, dream of me,
   And may your dreams ever pleasant be.
   Goodnight, dear, dream of me,
   And may your dreams ever pleasant be.
   *Goodnight, beloved (etc.)*

# Springtime blossom

Bulgarian

1. Spring-time blos-som beau-ti-fies the bow - ers, — Fair I - ri - na gath-ers pret - ty flow - ers, — Cher - ry blos - som, ho - ney suc - kle, — clo - ver, — All their per - fumes ri - vall - ing each o - ther. — o - ther. —

2. Fair Irina, with her flowing tresses,
Gathers flowers while the wind caresses.
‖: "Dearest Mitko, your true love awaits you;
Come back, Mitko,
let my arms embrace you. :‖

3. "Where, I wonder, is my lover roaming?
Why, I wonder, is no letter coming?
‖: Spring is lovers' time,
season of sweet passion;
Yet my maiden days
are quickly passing." :‖

4. Springtime blossom beautifies the bowers,
Fair Irina gathers pretty flowers;
‖: Gathers flowers, bitterly lamenting:
Budding branches
in the breeze are bending. :‖

5. From the branches
swoops a swallow, saying:
"I shall show you
where your love is staying."
‖: Off the bird flies and she follows after;
"Lead me," she cries,
"lead me to him faster." :‖

6. Here they buried him,
where the weeds grow thickly,
And an eagle guards his grave in pity,
‖: With his body warding off the weather,
Thus the eagle mourns the fallen rebel. :‖

# The miller's daughter

Bohemian

1. Down the stream so cheer-ful-ly Be-side the mill we row, Where the e-choes mer-ri-ly Their play-ful cho-rus throw. Tra la la la— la— la— la, La la la— la, La la la— la, Tra la la la— la— la— la, La— la la— la la, ———— To the pret-ty Na-ta-lie A

2. ‖: When we call, so readily
She answers us again;
Stops the wheel right steadily
To hear our homeward strain. :‖
*Tra la la la (etc)*

3. ‖: Parting then regretfully,
We pass the dark'ning hill;
Pretty, pretty maid, adieu,
And tic tac goes the mill. :‖
*Tra la la la (etc.)*

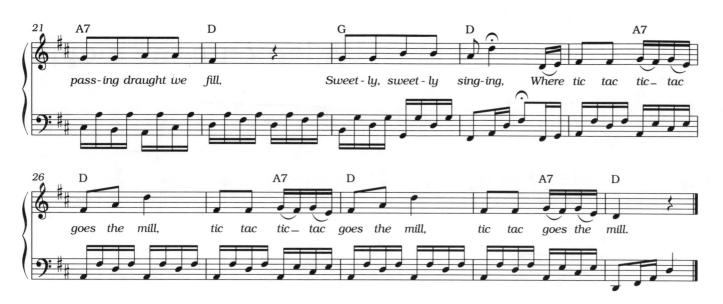

pass-ing draught we fill, Sweet-ly, sweet-ly sing-ing, Where tic tac tic_ tac

goes the mill, tic tac tic_ tac goes the mill, tic tac goes the mill.

# Here's a dance

**Brightly**

Serbian

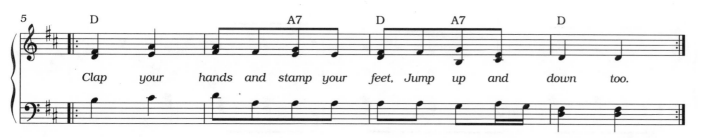

1. Here's a dance to dance, It's ve-ry ea-sy to do.

Clap your hands and stamp your feet, Jump up and down too.

2. You can all join in,
   And do it just like we do.
   *Clap your hands (etc.)*

3. If you like it tell your friends
   To do what you do.
   *Clap your hands (etc.)*

# Underneath the maple

Polish

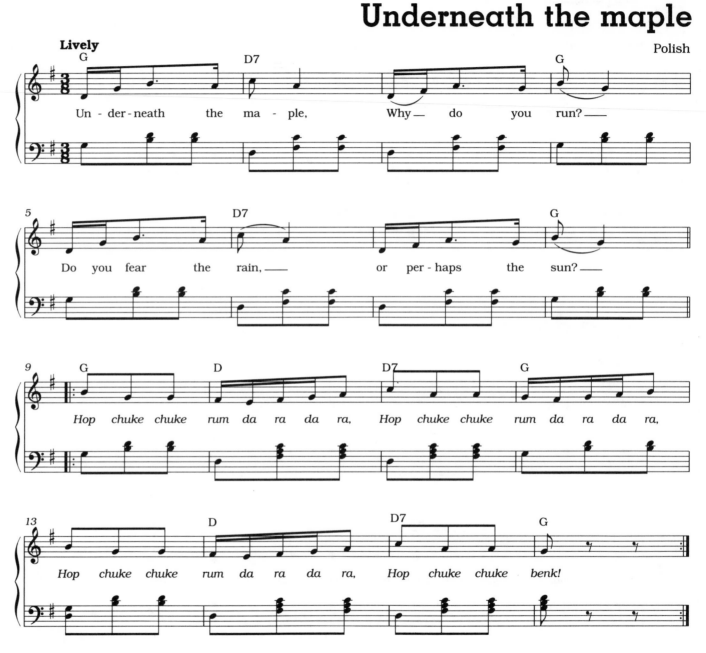

**Lively**

G · · · D7 · · · G
Un - der - neath the ma - ple, Why — do you run? —

5 · · · D7 · · · G
Do you fear the rain, — or per - haps the sun? —

9 G · · · D · · · D7 · · · G
Hop chuke chuke rum da ra da ra, Hop chuke chuke rum da ra da ra,

13 · · · D · · · D7 · · · G
Hop chuke chuke rum da ra da ra, Hop chuke chuke benk!

2. Underneath the maple
   Why do you cry?
   Don't you like it wet?
   Don't you like it dry?
   *Hop chuke chuke (etc.)*

# The Kolo

Croatian

Brightly

Stand in line and all join hands, Dance the spright-ly Ko - lo.

1. Stamp and hop, stamp and hop, Stamp and hop, stamp and hop,
2. Clap and hop, stamp clap and hop, Clap and hop, clap and hop,

Run - ning free, just fol - low me, And don't be first to stop, stop.

—21—

# Cradle song

Czech

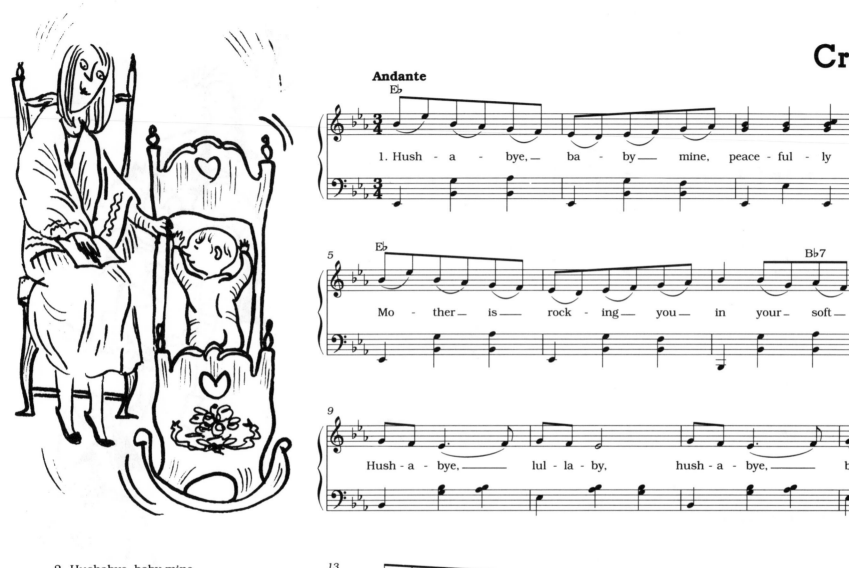

**Andante**

1. Hush - a - bye,— ba - by— mine, peace - ful - ly rest;

Mo - ther is— rock - ing— you— in your— soft— nest.

Hush - a - bye,———— lul - la - by, hush - a - bye,———— ba - by,

Mo - ther is— rock - ing— you— in your— soft— nest.

2. Hushabye, baby mine,
   dim grows the light;
   Close your eyes, go to sleep,
   darling, goodnight.
   Hushabye, lullaby,
   hushabye, baby,
   Close your eyes, go to sleep,
   darling, good night.

# On a Sunday morning

Polish

**Gaily**

1. On a Sun - day morn - - - - ing my young daugh - ter sang a song, Daugh - ter sang and so did I, We sang a song to - ge - ther, Daugh - ter sang and so did I, We sang a song to - ge - ther.

2. On a Monday morning
   My young daughter danced a dance.
   Daughter danced, and so did I,
   We danced a dance together,
   Daughter danced, and so did I,
   We danced a dance together.

# Soldier's song

Romanian

**March time**

1. On the path - - - - way through the valley, On the path-way through the val - ley Rode a sol - dier strong and man - ly: Oh, his life so cheer - ful and care - free!

2. On the pathway by the mountain,
On the pathway by the mountain
Rode a soldier strong and manly:
Oh, his life so cheerful and carefree!

3. On the pathway up the hillside,
On the pathway up the hillside
Rode a soldier strong and manly:
Oh, his life so cheerful and carefree!

# I ne'er went to my school late

Czech

**Brightly**

When I first to school was sent, I learnt how the
num - bers went: One and two, three and four,
I know these and ma - ny more. Five and six,
seven and eight, I ne'er went to my school late.

# May our Poland never perish

Polish national anthem

2. Though we're conquer'd
   by our neighbours,
   We still hurl defiance;
   Spartan breasts as strong as sabres,
   We have self-reliance.
   March, march, Dabrowski,
   March to Poland then from Italy:
   ‖: You give inspiration,
   To unite our nation. :‖

3. And the valour of our people
   Is an ancient story:
   It's proclaimed from ev'ry steeple,
   For we still have glory.
   March, march, Dabrowski,
   March to Poland then from Italy:
   ‖: Liberty is crying,
   But is far from dying. :‖

# Rocking

Czech

Gently

1. Lit - tle Je - sus, sweet - ly sleep, do not stir,
2. Ma - ry's lit - tle ba - by, sleep, sweet - ly sleep,

We will lend a coat of fur.
Sleep in com - fort slum - ber deep.

We will rock you, rock you, rock you,

we will rock you, rock you, rock you;

See the coat to
We will serve you

keep you warm, Snug - ly round your ti - ny form.
all we can, Dar - ling, dar - ling lit - tle man.

Reproduced from *The Oxford Book of Carols* by permission of Oxford University Press.

# The birds' carol

Czech

**Rather quick**

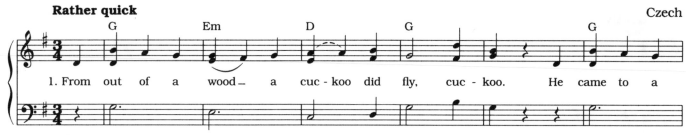

1. From out of a wood — a cuc-koo did fly, cuc-koo. He came to a

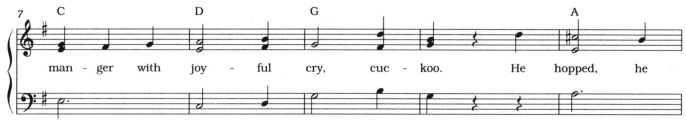

man - ger with joy - ful cry, cuc - koo. He hopped, he

curt - sied, round he flew, And loud his ju - bi -

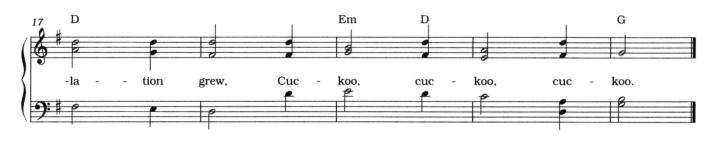

-la - - tion grew, Cuc - koo, cuc - koo, cuc - koo.

2. A pigeon flew over to Galilee, vrercroo;
   He strutted and cooed
      and was full of glee, vrercroo;
   He showed with jeweled wings unfurled
   His joy that Christ was in the world,
   Vrercroo, vrercroo, vrercroo.

3. A dove settled down
      upon Nazareth, tsucroo,
   And tenderly chanted
      with all his breath, tsucroo;
   "O you," he cooed, "so good and true,
   My beauty I do give to you."

# Infant holy, infant lowly

Polish